Landform Top Tens

The World's Most Amazing Rivers

Anita Ganeri

Raintree

Chicago, Illinois

www.heinemannraintree.com
Visit our website to find out
more information about
Heinemann-Raintree books.

To order:

☎ Phone 888-454-2279

🖥 Visit www.heinemannraintree.com
to browse our catalog and order online.

© 2009 Raintree
an imprint of Capstone Global Library, LLC
Chicago, Illinois

Customer Service: 888-454-2279

Visit our website at www.heinemannraintree.com

Edited by Louise Galpine, Kate DeVilliers,
and Rachel Howells
Designed by Victoria Bevan and Geoff Ward
Original illustrations © Capstone Global
Library Limited
Illustrated by Geoff Ward
Picture research by Hannah Taylor
Production by Alison Parsons

Printed and bound in China by CTPS

13 12 11 10 09
10 9 8 7 6 5 4 3 2 1

Library of Congress Cataloging-in-Publication Data

Ganeri, Anita, 1961-
  The world's most amazing rivers / Anita Ganeri.
    p. cm. -- (Landform top tens)
  Includes bibliographical references and index.
  ISBN 978-1-4109-3702-5 (hc) -- ISBN 978-1-4109-3710-0
(pb)
  1. Rivers--Juvenile literature. I. Title.
  GB1203.8.G36 2008
  551.48'3--dc22
                                2008051533

Acknowledgments

We would like to thank the following for permission
to reproduce photographs: Ardea.com p. **20** (Dae Sasitorn);
Art Directors p. **15** (Bob Turner); Corbis pp. **10** (Jim
Richardson), **11** (NASA), **27** (Layne Kennedy); FLPA pp. **6**
(Imagebroker / Rainer F. Steussloff/Intro), **26** (Imagebroker
/ KFS); Getty Images pp. **4–5** (Walter Bibikow); istockphoto
p. **14** (Kuzma); OnAsia.com p. **23** (Suthep Kritsanavarin);
Photolibrary pp. **7** (Meredith Castlegate), **9** (Imagestate/
Steve Vidler), **12** (OSF/ John Downer), **13** and **24–25**
(Robin Smith), **18** (JTB Photo), **21** (Robert Harding Travel/
Charles Bowman); Science Photo Library pp. **8** (M-SAT
LTD), **19** (Earth Satelite corporation); Sovfoto pp. **16–17**
(Xinhua); Still Pictures p. **22** (Joerg Boethling).

Background images by Capstone Global Library Ltd
(Debbie Rowe) and Photolibrary (Photodisc).

Cover photograph of the Yangtze River in Qutang Gorge,
reproduced with permission of Corbis (Xiaoyang Liu).

We would like to thank Nick Lapthorn for his invaluable
help in the preparation of this book.

Every effort has been made to contact copyright holders
of material reproduced in this book. Any omissions will
be rectified in subsequent printings if notice is given to
the publishers.

Contents

Some words are printed in bold, **like this.** You can find out what they mean by looking in the glossary on page 31.

Rivers

Most rivers start as small springs high on hills or mountains. The place where a river starts is called its source. At first, a river flows quickly and picks up rocks and boulders. These scrape away at the ground, carving out a V-shaped **valley**.

Fresh water

About three-quarters of Earth's surface is covered with water. But about 97 percent of it is salty and lies in the oceans. The rest is called fresh water. Some of it is frozen as ice or flows underground. Less than 1 percent of fresh water flows in rivers.

In the middle part of a river, the water flows more slowly. It curves from side to side in loops, called **meanders**. Water from the surrounding land drains into the river. This land is called the river's drainage basin. Finally, the river flows into the sea at its **mouth**.

Hundreds of plants and animals live in or near rivers. People have also made their homes on riverbanks for thousands of years. They use the water for drinking, watering crops, supplying factories, and for transportation.

The Danube River flows across Europe to the sea.

Nile

The Nile in Africa is the world's longest river. It flows for 6,695 km (4,160 miles) from its source near Lake Victoria (also known as Victoria Nyanza) on the **equator**. Then it heads northward through Africa to its **mouth** on the Mediterranean Sea. Where the river joins the sea, there is an enormous delta (see box).

River deltas

A delta is a triangular-shaped area of land at a river's mouth. It happens when a river drops its load of sand, mud, and clay as it flows into the sea.

Since ancient times, the Nile River has been used for transportation.

NILE

CONTINENT:
AFRICA

LENGTH:
6,695 KM
(4,160 MILES)

SOURCE:
STREAM FLOWING INTO
LAKE VICTORIA

DRAINAGE BASIN:
3,349,000 KM^2 (1,293,056 SQ MILES)

THAT'S AMAZING!
THE NILE RIVER STARTS AS
TWO RIVERS—THE WHITE NILE
AND THE BLUE NILE. THEY MEET
IN SUDAN. THEY GET THEIR
NAMES FROM THE COLOR
OF THEIR WATER.

The Aswan High **Dam** was built across the Nile River to supply water and power.

Ancient Egypt

Without the Nile River, the **civilization** of ancient Egypt could not have existed. Most of Egypt is dry, rocky desert. The river supplied the ancient Egyptians with precious water for drinking and farming.

Amazon

The Amazon is the biggest river on Earth. It carries more water than any other river— about one-fifth of all river water. The river begins high up in the Andes Mountains in Peru. It then flows across South America to its **mouth** on the Atlantic Ocean. The Amazon drains an area about three-quarters of the size of the United States and has at least 1,000 known **tributaries**.

At the mouth of the Amazon, fresh river water flows miles out to sea (the blue area).

AMAZON

CONTINENT:
SOUTH AMERICA

LENGTH:
6,400 KM (3,976 MILES)

SOURCE:
ANDES MOUNTAINS

DRAINAGE BASIN:
7,050,000 KM² (2,722,020 SQ MILES)

THAT'S AMAZING!
AT THE MOUTH OF THE AMAZON, ABOUT 70 SWIMMING POOLS' WORTH OF FRESH RIVER WATER FLOWS INTO THE SEA EVERY SECOND.

Amazon

Pacific Ocean

SOUTH AMERICA

Atlantic Ocean

Amazon rain forest

The world's largest **rain forest** grows along the banks of the Amazon River. It covers around 6 million km² (2,316,000 sq miles) of land, which is almost the size of Australia. Thousands of species of plants and animals live in the rain forest. It is also home to groups of **indigenous** people who live by farming, hunting, and fishing in the river.

Many rain forest animals rely on the river for water and food.

Mississippi

The Mississippi River is one of the longest rivers in the United States. From its source in Lake Itasca in Minnesota, it flows for 3,780 km (2,348 miles) to its delta in the Gulf of Mexico. The Mississippi is one of the world's busiest rivers. It has been an important waterway for passenger and cargo boats for hundreds of years.

Paddle steamers were designed for use in the shallow waters of the Mississippi.

MISSISSIPPI

CONTINENT:
NORTH AMERICA

LENGTH:
3,780 KM (2,348 MILES)

SOURCE:
LAKE ITASCA

DRAINAGE BASIN:
3,256,000 KM² (1,257,148 SQ MILES)

THAT'S AMAZING!
THE MISSISSIPPI'S MANY NICKNAMES INCLUDE "OL' MAN RIVER" AND "OLD BLUE."

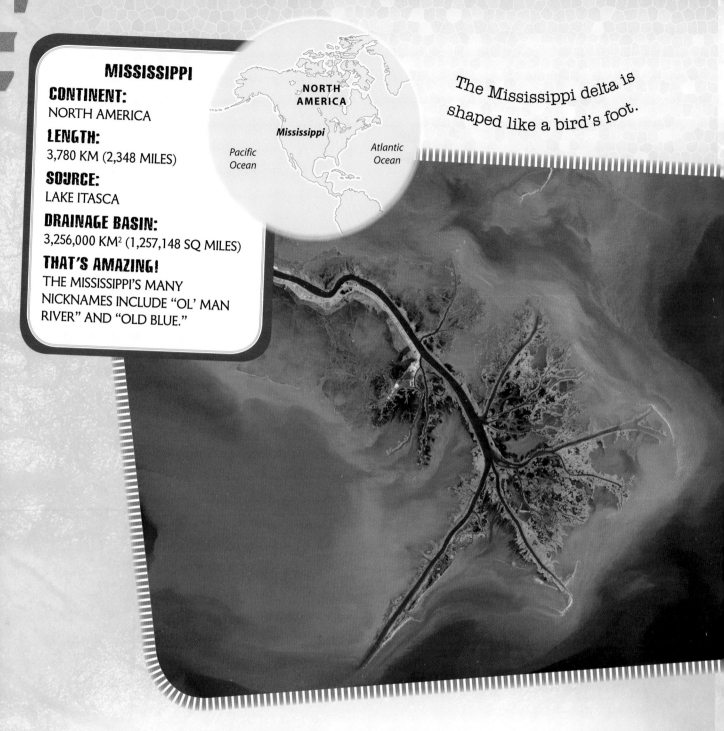

NORTH AMERICA

Mississippi

Pacific Ocean

Atlantic Ocean

The Mississippi delta is shaped like a bird's foot.

River transportation

Parts of the river are difficult to **navigate** because of **rapids**, shallow water, and rocks. Today, a system of **locks** and **dams** allows ships to bypass these obstacles.

Zambezi

From its source in Zambia, the Zambezi River flows through six countries on its way to the Indian Ocean. It is one of the longest rivers in Africa.

The Kariba Dam is 579 meters (1,900 feet) long and 128 meters (420 feet) high.

River power

The massive Kariba **Dam** on the Zambezi opened in 1959. It blocks the river and forms a **reservoir**, called Lake Kariba. The water in the reservoir is used to make electricity for Zambia and Zimbabwe. This type of electricity is called **hydroelectricity**.

ZAMBEZI

CONTINENT:
AFRICA

LENGTH:
2,754 KM (1,710 MILES)

SOURCE:
NEAR MWINILUNGA, ZAMBIA

DRAINAGE BASIN:
1,390,000 KM^2 (536,682 SQ MILES)

THAT'S AMAZING!
BULL SHARKS NORMALLY LIVE ALONG THE COAST, BUT THEY SOMETIMES SWIM UP LARGE RIVERS, INCLUDING THE ZAMBEZI.

AFRICA

Indian
Ocean

Atlantic
Ocean

Zambezi

The Victoria Falls on the Zambezi River is one of the world's largest waterfalls.

Victoria Falls

The Zambezi is world famous for the spectacular Victoria Falls, on the border between Zambia and Zimbabwe. Here the river plunges 108 meters (354 feet) over a cliff. In the local language, the Falls are called "Mosi-oa-Tunya" ("the smoke that thunders") because of the thunderous roar the water makes. Large numbers of crocodiles and hippopotamuses live in the river above the falls.

Volga

The Volga is the longest river in Europe. It flows through Russia from its source in the Valdai Hills to its **mouth** in the Caspian Sea. Where the Volga meets the sea, it forms a delta 160 km (100 miles) long, with hundreds of islands and **channels**. The delta is the only place in Europe where pelicans and flamingoes are found in their natural **habitat**.

For three months of winter, much of the Volga freezes over.

VOLGA

CONTINENT:
EUROPE

LENGTH:
3,530 KM (2,193 MILES)

SOURCE:
VALDAI HILLS

DRAINAGE BASIN:
1,350,000 KM^2 (521,237 SQ MILES)

THAT'S AMAZING!
MORE THAN HALF OF RUSSIA'S BIGGEST CITIES ARE LOCATED ON THE BANKS OF THE VOLGA.

Volga

EUROPE

Caspian Sea

The Moscow Canal links the city of Moscow to the Volga River.

River for trade

The Volga is very important for trade and transportation. In some places the river has been made wider so that larger ships, carrying oil and grains, can pass through. The Moscow Canal joins Moscow to the Volga, linking the city to five seas—the White Sea, Baltic Sea, Caspian Sea, Black Sea, and Sea of Azov. This gives a huge network for trade and transportation.

Yangtze

The source of the Yangtze is a **glacier** high in the mountains of northwest China. From there, it flows for 6,418 km (3,987 miles) to the East China Sea (part of the Pacific Ocean). The Yangtze is the longest river in Asia and the third-longest in the world. In Chinese, it is known as Chang Jiang, which means "Long River."

Melted snow trickles down mountain glaciers, finally reaching the Yangtze.

YANGTZE

CONTINENT:
ASIA

LENGTH:
6,418 KM (3,987 MILES)

SOURCE:
MOUNT GELANDANDONG

DRAINAGE BASIN:
1,683,500 KM^2 (650,000 SQ MILES)

THAT'S AMAZING!
ABOUT 25 **BILLION** TONS OF WASTE IS DUMPED INTO THE YANGTZE EACH YEAR, MAKING IT ONE OF THE WORLD'S MOST **POLLUTED** RIVERS.

ASIA

Yangtze

Pacific Ocean

Indian Ocean

Life along the river

The vast, flat **floodplain** of the Yangtze is China's richest farmland, ideal for growing rice, wheat, and cotton. The region is home to around 300 million people—about a quarter of China's population.

Flood alert

During the rainy season, the Yangtze can burst its banks and flood. Floods ruin crops and bring disaster for people living on the floodplain. In the 1998 floods, more than 3,000 people died and millions were made homeless.

Ganges

For **Hindus**, the Ganges River in India is a special river. The holy city of Varanasi stands on the riverbank. Each year, millions of Hindus visit Varanasi to bathe in the river. They believe that this will wash away their sins. They worship the river as the goddess Ganga.

GANGES

CONTINENT:
ASIA

LENGTH:
2,510 KM (1,560 MILES)

SOURCE:
GANGOTRI GLACIER

DRAINAGE BASIN:
975,900 KM² (376,797 SQ MILES)

THAT'S AMAZING!
ABOUT HALF A **BILLION** PEOPLE LIVE AND FARM ON THE GANGES **FLOODPLAIN**.

ASIA

Ganges

Pacific Ocean

Indian Ocean

Hindus bathe in the Ganges River at Varanasi, India.

The Ganges-Brahmaputra delta is shown here, in blue.

Ganges flow

The Ganges begins high in the Himalayas mountain range. Melting ice and snow from the Gangotri **glacier** trickles into a stream that joins with other streams to form the Ganges. The river then travels across northeast India and into Bangladesh. It flows into the Indian Ocean at the Bay of Bengal. There, it joins the Brahmaputra River to form the world's largest delta.

Thames

The Thames River is the longest river that flows entirely in England. It begins at Thames Head in Gloucestershire and flows across southern England into the North Sea. From London, the Thames is a tidal river. This means that its level rises and falls twice a day with the **tides** of the North Sea.

From its source, the Thames flows gently through the countryside.

THAMES

CONTINENT:
EUROPE

LENGTH:
346 KM (215 MILES)

SOURCE:
THAMES HEAD

DRAINAGE BASIN:
13,600 KM² (5,250 SQ MILES)

THAT'S AMAZING!
HUNDREDS OF YEARS AGO, THE THAMES SOMETIMES FROZE OVER IN WINTER. FROM 1564 AMUSEMENT PARKS WERE MADE ON THE ICE. THE LAST PARK WAS MADE IN 1814.

North
Sea

Thames

EUROPE

The port of London

The Thames is a famous river because it flows through London, the capital of England. London's position on the Thames made it an ideal site for a **port**. By the 1930s, London was the world's busiest port. Today, it is still one of the United Kingdom's main ports.

Estuaries

The Thames is a river that ends in an estuary, rather than a delta (see page 6). An estuary is the wide, lower section of a river where the tides flow in and out from the sea.

Many famous London buildings, such as the Houses of Parliament, stand on the banks of the Thames.

Mekong

The Mekong, one of the longest rivers in Asia, flows through six countries on its journey from its source to the sea. It begins as a spring in the mountains of northwest China and reaches the sea at a vast delta in Vietnam. In the upper part of the Mekong, the water is clear and fast-flowing. Later, it turns rusty-red from the soil it carries along.

These flooded rice paddy fields are along the banks of the Mekong.

MEKONG

CONTINENT:
ASIA

LENGTH:
4,350 KM (2,703 MILES)

SOURCE:
LASAGONGMA SPRING

DRAINAGE BASIN:
795,000 KM² (306,951 SQ MILES)

THAT'S AMAZING!
SEVERAL TYPES OF GIANT FISH
LIVE IN THE RIVER, INCLUDING
GIANT CATFISH AND RIVER CARP
UP TO 3 METERS (10 FEET) LONG.

ASIA

Mekong

Pacific
Ocean

Indian
Ocean

Giant catfish can be
caught in the Mekong.

River resources

Millions of people live along the river and rely on it
for food to eat and sell. The Mekong delta is one of the
world's richest rice-growing areas. Farmers in the delta
also catch many types of fish, such as catfish. They build
their houses on stilts over the river and feed the fish
to fatten them up.

Murray

The Murray River is the largest river in Australia. It begins in the Australian Alps, then flows across southeast Australia to its **mouth** in the Indian Ocean. At the mouth, **dredging machines** dig sand from a **channel** to stop the mouth from becoming clogged. The Murray joins the Darling River at the town of Wentworth to form the huge Murray-Darling river system.

Water levels

Australia is a hot, dry country with little rainfall. These conditions mean great changes in the amount of water flowing in the Murray at different times of the year. In times of extreme **drought**, the river has even been known to dry up completely, although this is very rare. In times of heavy rain, the river can flood.

Wentworth is the place where the Murray and Darling Rivers join.

MURRAY

CONTINENT:
AUSTRALASIA

LENGTH:
2,575 KM (1,600 MILES)

SOURCE:
AUSTRALIAN ALPS

DRAINAGE BASIN:
1,061,469 KM² (409,835 SQ MILES)

THAT'S AMAZING!
IN **ABORIGINAL** MYTH, THE MURRAY WAS CREATED FROM THE TRACKS OF A HUNTER CHASING A GIANT FISH.

AUSTRALASIA

Indian Ocean

Pacific Ocean

AUSTRALIA

Murray

Rivers in Danger

All over the world, rivers are in danger. The main reason is **pollution,** caused by sewage, factory waste, and chemicals washed off farmers' fields. Pollution kills river animals and plants, and it makes the water too dirty and dangerous for people to use.

Hundreds of factories have been built along the banks of the Rhine River in Europe. They use the river for transportation, and for water for making goods. But they also pump poisonous waste into the river, with disastrous effects.

Factories along the Rhine pump dangerous wastes into the water.

By the 1970s, the Rhine was so dirty that it was called the "sewer of Europe." An international campaign was launched to clean up the river. Today, species of fish, such as salmon, are returning to the river after many years away.

Members of the Mississippi River Beautification and Restoration Project remove refrigerators, barrels, and tires from the Mississippi River.

Hope for the future

Conservation groups are working hard to save the world's rivers. Each year, tens of thousands of helpers in the United States take part in the National River Cleanup. In 2007 they cleaned almost 12,070 km (7,500 miles) of river and collected 540 tonnes (600 tons) of garbage. Amazingly, this included washing machines and lawnmowers dumped in the rivers.

River Facts and Figures

Rivers run through almost every country. They often begin in mountains, flowing from **glaciers**, lakes, and springs. They shape the landscape, in some places cutting deep **valleys** and high waterfalls. In other places, they create vast **floodplains** and deltas. Which river do you think is the most amazing?

This map of the world shows all the rivers described in this book.

Arctic Ocean

NORTH AMERICA

Mississippi

Thames **EUROPE**

Volga **ASIA**

Atlantic Ocean

Nile

Ganges

Yangtze

AFRICA

Mekong

Pacific Ocean

Amazon

SOUTH AMERICA

Zambezi

Indian Ocean

AUSTRALASIA

Pacific Ocean

Murray

Southern Ocean

ANTARCTICA

NILE

LENGTH:
6,695 KM (4,160 MILES)

SOURCE:
LAKE VICTORIA

DRAINAGE BASIN:
3,349,000 KM^2
(1,293,056 SQ MILES)

AMAZON

LENGTH:
6,400 KM (3,976 MILES)

SOURCE:
ANDES MOUNTAINS

DRAINAGE BASIN:
7,050,000 KM^2
(2,722,020 SQ MILES)

MISSISSIPPI

LENGTH:
3,780 KM (2,348 MILES)

SOURCE:
LAKE ITASCA

DRAINAGE BASIN:
3,256,000 KM^2
(1,257,148 SQ MILES)

ZAMBEZI

LENGTH:
2,754 KM (1,710 MILES)

SOURCE:
NEAR MWINILUNGA, ZAMBIA

DRAINAGE BASIN:
1,390,000 KM^2
(536,682 SQ MILES)

VOLGA

LENGTH:
3,530 KM (2,193 MILES)

SOURCE:
VALDAI HILLS

DRAINAGE BASIN:
1,350,000 KM^2
(521,237 SQ MILES)

YANGTZE

LENGTH:
6,418 KM (3,987 MILES)

SOURCE:
MOUNT GELANDANDONG

DRAINAGE BASIN:
1,683,500 KM^2
(650,000 SQ MILES)

GANGES

LENGTH:
2,510 KM (1,560 MILES)

SOURCE:
GANGOTRI GLACIER

DRAINAGE BASIN:
975,900 KM^2
(376,797 SQ MILES)

THAMES

LENGTH:
346 KM (215 MILES)

SOURCE:
THAMES HEAD

DRAINAGE BASIN:
13,600 KM^2
(5,250 SQ MILES)

MEKONG

LENGTH:
4,350 KM (2,703 MILES)

SOURCE:
LASAGONGMA SPRING

DRAINAGE BASIN:
795,000 KM^2
(306,951 SQ MILES)

MURRAY

LENGTH:
2,575 KM (1,600 MILES)

SOURCE:
AUSTRALIAN ALPS

DRAINAGE BASIN:
1,061,469 KM^2
(409,835 SQ MILES)

Find Out More

Books to read

Chambers, Catherine, and Nicholas Lapthorn. *Mapping Earthforms: Rivers*. Chicago: Heinemann Library, 2008.

Ganeri, Anita. *Horrible Geography: Raging Rivers and Odious Oceans*. New York: Scholastic, 2001.

Morris, Neil. *Landscapes and People: Earth's Changing Rivers*. Chicago: Raintree, 2004.

Spilsbury, Louise, and Richard Spilsbury. *World Cultures: Living on the Ganges River*. Chicago: Raintree, 2008.

Websites

National Geographic

www.nationalgeographic.com/geography-action/rivers.html

Use this web page to find maps, activities, videos, and more about rivers.

National River Cleanup

www.americanrivers.org

Find out about the National River Cleanup and what to do if you want to organize a cleanup of your own.

Rivernet

www.rivernet.org/rivers.htm

Find out more about rivers of the world and the environmental impact of **dam** building.

Glossary

Aboriginal to do with the Aborigines, the people who originally lived in Australia

Australasia term used to describe Australia, New Zealand, and a series of nearby islands in the Pacific Ocean

billion thousand million

channel narrow passage of water

civilization group of people with a highly developed culture and way of life

conservation protecting threatened animals and habitats

dam barrier built across a river to form a reservoir

dredging machine machine used to scoop or dig soil from a riverbed

drought water shortage caused by a lack of rain

equator imaginary line around the middle of Earth

floodplain flat area around a river, formed from soil dumped when the river floods

glacier river of ice that flows slowly down a mountain

habitat where a plant or animal lives

Hindu person who follows Hinduism

hydroelectricity electricity that uses the power of running water

indigenous person who originally comes from a place

lock part of a river that can be closed off by gates to control the water level

meander horseshoe-shaped bend in a river

mouth opening where a river flows into the sea

navigate find the way

pollution waste and dirt that can damage Earth

port town along a river or near the sea where ships can be loaded and unloaded

rain forest thick forest growing around the equator where the climate is hot and wet

rapid part of a river where the water is very fast-flowing

reservoir lake formed when a dam is built across a river

tide change in sea level caused by the pulling force of the Moon and Sun

tributary small river that flows into another bigger river or lake

valley long, V-shaped dip in the ground, carved out by a river

Index